THE DEATH OF A CLOWN

C000021364

Tom Bland studied psychotherapy and dream analysis at the Society for Psychology and Healing, and is completing an MA in Contemporary Performance Practices at the University of East London. He edited the online poetry magazine, *Blue of Noon*, which published risk-taking and provocative work. He is writing his first collection and devising live art performances.

Death of a Clown

Published by Bad Betty Press in 2018
www.badbettypress.com

Cover design by Amy Acre

Printed and bound in the United Kingdom

A CIP record of this book is available from the British Library.

ISBN: 978-1-9997147-5-8

The Death of a
TOM Clown
BLAND

PRESS

Love is like a brick. You can build a house or sink a dead body.

– Lady Gaga

The Death of a Clown

*To a good friend, K, who helped me
in an unsettling time.*

You reminded me
of my old boss,
a sexologist who snorted coke
and undressed in front of me
in the kitchen,

then ran into the street
knocking off a policeman's helmet.

Why is ritual so important?

'I promise to love you,' Tracey Emin writes in a heart.
It isn't a real heart;
it doesn't even look like a real one.

                        Electric neon.
                        The first sketch
drawn in black ink on a sheet of textured paper, and then
                        ?

a burst
of
red light. In the workshop
in Bethnal Green. It isn't a real heart; it doesn't even
that time I had a pig's heart in my mouth running
around the stage
at the Roundhouse.
                        It tasted of sick.

The clown teacher examined my outstretched hands, then remarked,
'Do you think we are stupid? We KNOW there isn't a box in your hands.'
            I felt ashamed.
            As I sat back down, the student next to me said,
'No matter. Try Again. *Fail* again. *Fail* better.'
            I knew who he was quoting
but instead of shouting it out, I just kissed him, like in the pub last night.
After a pint, he stroked my inner thigh, my tongue naturally slipped into
his mouth. Our tongues.
            Fuck him. Everyone watching.

Bob Rogers always began the Sufi circle with, 'The goal here is
        to
     create and destroy
     the idols of the self,' then he glared at me,
'but this is not an apocalyptic vision.' At first, this unnerved me,
but quickly, it started to annoy me, so much so, I had printed on
        pink badges,
a feminine figure and the words,
     LIFE IS DEATH.
I gave the badges
        out to the group to their discomfort
and/or amusement. He asked me to leave. He said, 'Sufism isn't
     about death but a new beginning.'

Once a year, *The Guardian* has the headline
in their ever-shrinking culture section,

AUTOBIOGRAPHY IS DEAD.

One day soon, when language and experience
have
finally reached their divorce settlement,
words will only be words.

'Oh shit, does that mean poetry is dead too?' my
friend said, almost breaking one of his teeth opening
Weston's Old Rosie, which he poured
into a glass of brandy and brown sugar
to kill memory – any memory.
'You can't experience anything with memory holding you
back,' he said, spitting out the lid.

*

I was standing outside a Dalston
club, when a woman
in a monochrome dress asked me
what my greatest achievement
was to date. I replied, 'Learning to speak.'

*

I was born
constricted with the umbilical twisted around my neck and torso –
born
dead. Oxygen-brain-activity-electrical-language
terminated for a pinpoint second.

MY MOUTH>MY BRAIN>CONNECTION>DISJOINTED.

As a child, I only spoke
to myself. In my head. Only I knew what I meant.
I had to learn how to say things. Sounds into words.
Actual words others understood.

                    *

About a year ago, I found myself
snorting lines of coke,
but I hated doing it with other people,
only alone.
Blue in the face.
Breathing blue.
Heart racing.
Near heart attack. Was this orgasm? Was I even hard?

I loved the intensity of being on my own –

my adrenaline induced
out of body
looking back at my pulsating limbs;
that self-aware speck

jittering or jumping between the two,
like
being dead/born once again.

Ranting so fast all my words blurred into rapid
hand gestures, the very
shapes of my early tongue-tied jabbering.

                    *

Outside
the Dalston club,
she blew a smoke ring,
throwing
the butt on the floor.
I took
a long drag
on my own cig. 'You
speak ok now though,'
she said,
rubbing her head.

Amy was a clown,
describing herself as an acid maverick pioneering
the eye in the triangle she wore around her neck
falling onto the bright green t-shirt. 'Clowning's
a cult,' she said, opening
an empty
envelope sitting between her almost finished espresso
and her latex red nose. 'Some
people think the clown is a performance I put on
and take off, but no, I *must* be a clown
at all times. I can't stand slipping back
into *that thing…*'

HUMAN.

I met
Amy on a three-week clown retreat in
the cider brewing region
of Hertfordshire, surrounded by trees and red noses,
crisscrossing between technical mime exercises
and the spontaneous scream
from the bowels upward.
'Don't be afraid to scream, Tom,'
she said/I said to myself.

She reminded me too much of myself,
that made me scream,
seeing myself as a blond-haired woman with
the perfect pear-shaped figure

standing in front of me
wearing her red nose,
laughing
poking me
hitting me (with a rubber machete)
telling me
to *wake up!* –
she,
an acidic
Osho
in a polka dot outfit
screaming,

THE
GOLDEN
REALITY
WILL
DAWN
IN
YOU
MOTHER
FUCKER.

*

There was a clown
who was also a serial killer,
but he never killed as a clown.

When he scrubbed away the makeup,
bits of his stubble came out;
his teeth gripped,
trying to hold in the impulse
to kill.

He stared at himself in the mirror,
at the face
he was born with.

In his red book, he wrote,
'Sadness,
that feeling in
me
terrifies me, only stripping it away
in the bodies of others –
the cute young men in Converse
trainers –
makes the void something I can step into again.'
I imagined
being killed by him.

Amy took on his role
slicing away the sadness in me until my face shone so wide,
she could see my teeth in the sunshine
awkwardly appearing between the beech trees,
squirting ketchup on me
to make it all seem
real.

We decided to swap clothes,
to be each other, at dinner in front of all the other clowns.
She ate steak
and I ate potatoes and both of us had onion sauce
on silver plates, and some clowns thought we
had been fucking
but I shouted, 'She was killing me for my own good!'

The next day
she looked at me
and said, 'Darling, don't
you wanna kill me?'
Straight out of nowhere,
I slammed the rubber machete
into her heart, whispering in her ear,
'I too dream of love.'

But
we
both
just
laughed.

The man behind
the counter offered me
onion rings
instead of the cardboard cut-out skinny fries.
I swamped them in
barbecue sauce downing vanilla Coke to take away the
ketchup base taste.

Unwrapping
the succulent
Double
Whopper with my teeth
in front of the full
length windows
through
which I saw
everyone walking.

Out of the haze of
Taylor Swift,
young people crammed in, just out of college,
being forced education like a virus. A deadly boring one.
I heard,

THE END TIMES ARE HERE: SINNERS REPENT,

coming out of an iPhone
swinging
out of a handbag.

I was flicking through
Edward Edinger's last work where he analysed
the cult of the apocalypse as a psychological myth
of the disintegrating self:

that black hole
undoing
the whole goddamn
personality
machine. I felt like
a robot;

pre-programmed,

pre-designed,

and god had fucked-up the first human.

Adam, a fragmented template,

a disaster waiting to happen.

The onion rings
had that quintessential crunch
even though one of my canines broke
last year when I had a Stella glass
thrown at me
so the dentist pulled out the root.
I bled a lot.
Down my chin. Into the bib. Over the latex glove.

I told my therapist I often disintegrate. I wrote
down all my thoughts to find where they all came from,

but I ended up smashing my phone and
burning pages and insulting people on street corners.

In St Paul, 'I die daily,'
In Muhammad, 'Die before you die,'
In Jesus, 'I came to bring a sword,'
these
things,
in
my mind,
blaring out,

24 hours a day like

a radio tower
just repeating DIE –
any kind of death –

like the

old Russian tower

seemingly broadcasting mindless noise
but we know it's still set – waiting/on tenterhooks –
to receive

the correct
Soviet
code
to activate THE BOMB.

*

My therapist analysed one of my dreams
of a revolution I watched with a lover/a substitute
mother, and in response, he said, 'Rarely do revolutions
work, they never achieve their transformative
potential.'

He was telling me
not to end my life
('Strangulation IS the best method,'
I said to shock
him)

but when I fall in love

(a virus of nature twisting
itself out of shape/pretence
of the divine/god is dead)

I plan
my funeral –
Lady Gaga
will sing 'The Edge of Glory' over a

huge bonfire. My corpse in a coffin will be on top and
her suspension wires will accidentally snap. She will fall
straight onto me.
My therapist said,
'You project a lot.'
His therapy
room was on the top floor of a Victorian house
where I sat opposite the window. I could
see
the top half

of a weeping willow.

Amy told me
masturbating was not the same as
meditating. But the cult
of masturbation had already
found its way into ... *no one can make*
you come like yourself ... a manifesto
of poetic intent. Millions
of potential lives
wiped away in a tissue down the toilet drain.

*

I had this dream of my teenage
bedroom, where two wardrobes
swapped themselves around,

revealing a hole
where a spider went down to a room –
a museum –

beneath mine,

exhibiting foetuses
in jars of formaldehyde
on white pillars.

The tour guide
touched one of the visitors,
feeling his spine
through the heavy wool coat.

A copy of Colin Wilson's
serial killer book
coming out of the pocket.

On the front cover, a photo
of Ted Bundy
holding an orange balloon.

All of a sudden,
Gregg Araki burst into the museum,
proclaiming,

LIFE IS LONELY AND BORING
AND DUMB,

which everyone knew was a line
from one of his films, but they all
clapped anyway, throwing glitter over him.

I remembered
the words inside
Wilson's book,

KILLING
IS THE LONELIEST CULT,

someone had scrawled
on every page
of my secondhand copy.

*

'I was already a clown but never a serial killer
despite the amount of sperm I threw away,'
I scribbled on an A3 cardboard sheet.

*

'I became obsessed with psychopaths when I realised
killing to them was a language,'
my then boss, Dr Zoe Gemini, voiced
rehearsing for an interview with *The Daily Telegraph*,
'they were discovering
its complex
semantics each time
they cut into the screaming bodies
in their soundproof steel-bolted basements.'

I was sitting on the edge of her bed attempting
to find where she had lost a thousand pounds,
which she was sure was in her Versace handbag
until I looked inside
and found another empty Versace bag. She stormed in
throwing
the bags against the wall
yelling at me,
'Therapy's about learning to speak
the strangeness with the whole of your mouth.'

*

The clown/killer (but never at the same time)
left a large machine gun toting figurine propped up
in a rain-filled pothole. He wrote on the street,

CLOWN'S A FOREIGNER IN A FUCKED-
UP(sidedown)LAND

'Tom, what do you want?'
Amy asked,
squeezing my elbow a little too tight.

*

Gregg Araki pulled the chain attached to the clown/killer's neck,
forcing him into the museum,
where he stood
exposing his genitals from behind his hands
to the visitors asking his name and taking a stream
of photos.

Before his execution, he learnt to paint;
he loved painting as much as killing. He painted Elvis from
a photo in the prison's copy of *Teen Magazine*.

Supposedly his last
words were, 'We are children wearing the masks of adults.'

*

I had never been good with feelings – they seemed
alien, possessed by others – until I looked
in the mirror wearing a red nose. It enlarged
every
facial expression
causing ecstatic emotions to roll through me,
but it seemed
like folly
to say I was human.
I performed
naked in front of 300 people but I performed off the stage
to the side, so they each decided whether

to see me.

                    *

Dr Zoe Gemini asked me
to check whether she had any Tampax
in the bathroom
but all I found was a copy of *The Satanic Bible*. She said,
'Oh, that's a cute cult of narcissism.' She had seen
my drawings of
hermaphrodites I studied from medical textbooks.
She asked me
whether I was truly male.

                    *

In *post-it-notes-on-serial-killing*,
Dr Zoe Gemini poeticised, 'Women viscerally
sense death –
all the failed lives –
the ones never born:
an insight
men will never get from their sperm; too much like
liquid plastic
over the face of a barbie doll *to be* pain.'

At 13,
I cut out images
from *Hello* magazine and glued them over
the inside pages of library books.

In the park, somebody
left polaroids
of a gagged woman bound on a mattress
inside a van. As I discovered them
under the hawthorn, I

felt eyes
watching me. I ran under the bridge
back into the shopping centre.

I WAS A MESSED UP KID,

as I painted years later
on a t-shirt for the Frieze Art Fair, only to find out
words weren't hip anymore.

Michelle called pain (her pain) the sun god Ra.
Ra equalled pathos. Heat. She asked the question
how can life – let alone love – exist

in this fucked up world? in her own words,
a book I loved.

I didn't know I
was meant to give my pathos a
name. It was too secret, but she squeezed it out,
like when we did such bad coke
our noses bled into kisses –

we mixed our brains in a bowl of trash-poetry.

She quoted D. H. Lawrence around the edges,
his secret Ra magic, 'poetry the living chaos stirs,
sun-suffused and sun-impulsive, and most subtly chaotic,'
her lips
shivered/our minds glistened.
'I love the stories of the young man Jesus,' I said
kissing her on the lips. 'Who hasn't fantasised
about being sacrificed to the sun god?'

The death card fell
in front of me, the one
the sun-god lays down
to end
a zigzag fate
of a misspent life;

my kind of life, but not mine, not this time.
One of us broke my new belt –
it was only five pounds
from the Heart Foundation –
it was either me whipping her backside
or she strangling me. Or both.

Just words, just pain, the Blood Jesus finally appeared to me

in a hotel room

crucified to the neon red Christmas tree –

that red
on blazing red
no one ever
spoke about. A plastic angel on top. She was fast asleep.

She wanted to cut me, implant a terrifying thought in my body,
not heart, not there, nearer the shoulder, nearer to my ear,
she couldn't sleep for more than an hour in my bed; she couldn't
let me sleep for more than an hour in hers.
Only in a hotel room did she feel somewhat safe. I was tonic
(but not enough) and she was delirium
(my head almost exploded) as she wrapped the belt
around my neck, the first night we met.
She pulled so tight, my face turned bluish purple.
When I came I was still hard, but I had to squeeze her hands free,
otherwise the belt would have killed me.

The next time she stayed with her husband,
she hid herself in the attic and
tried to kill herself. She forced pills down her throat,
before hanging
herself from the ceiling.

Her husband slapped/shouted/woke her up,
and took her to the hospital, saving her
life, then he walked out leaving her alone on the bed.

I didn't know what to say, so I just listened to
her perturbed speech on the
phone before I explained how to escape sectioning.

And that card, the tower, fell in front of me;
the two lost souls, one falling head first, the other impaled
on the spiked walls.

I sat for an hour staring at her pink book,
before she called again but I remained still,
outside on my steps, looking up at the moon.

Sometimes I call my pain Hekate.

In Fuz Sxx, the shop assistant and I watched a man
masturbating over a blow-up doll. He came over the lips.

The shop assistant was a 20-something
in a black t-shirt and jeans. I too was in black.

The man suddenly looked up, realising we were there,
his trousers fell down
around his ankles; he fell over them

onto the orange-brown carpet
still with the same dirt from the 1980s.

I felt slightly sick, slightly amused, slightly excited,
and she, stroking her belly button ring
over the black t-shirt, she looked slightly disgusted.

His buttocks
reaching up, his knees on the ground,
his semi-erection dangling,

rolling it back into his underpants, she said,
'He's such a weirdo. He never speaks to anyone.'

*

In Hard, I watched a skinhead in the doggy position
being fucked
by another skinhead in Grinders boots.

A leather queen refused to show me
how to use the ball-crushing device he had in his hand
saying my balls were too pink to know such pain,

but then he started telling me
about gay serial killers.
I pinched his nipple when he mentioned

chopping up body parts for the acid bath. He ran
out of the club terrified of me.

    *

'Have you ever tried on a pair of knickers?'
she asked, pointing at the shop's

railing of Satin and PVC G-strings.
'So many men buy
them and insist they are for their girlfriends.'

    *

In one of the bedrooms, Sarah and I
were talking, and everyone else was downstairs
attempting to do speed, not knowing

if it was on the gums or up the nose.
I told her about the man who had tied me to a chair,

clamping my foreskin, pushing the
needle through the left and then the right side
in an act of ritual piercing. She stretched

out the foreskin with her teeth on the rings.
Her friend burst in shouting at me.

*

'I like wearing silk boxers. I have
a floral pair on today,' I said,
just showing her the top of them.

'I like your hair,' she said, 'it's very androgynous.
I dated a girl who looked like you. She was a cross between
a goth and a hippie. Do you like girls?'

*

He was on his knees,
squeezing my arse, sucking my cock, his fingers going inside.

*

I, on my knees, in front of her, kissing through her knickers.
She slipped them down, opening herself up,
simultaneously

pulling on my hair, screaming, 'Go right inside the hole.'
She pushed my body down onto the ground.
sliding my cock in, forcing her knickers into my mouth,

but then she asked, 'Are you actually going to buy anything?'
I handed over the RE/Search book, *Modern Primitives*, which
she placed in a paper bag. 'I read a survey suggesting

60% of sex shop users
reuse the plastic bags for auto-erotic-asphyxiation, sometimes
their eyeballs pop, or they just die.'

I was lying on my bed, seemingly
without any bones, when I
first saw on YouTube
the axe-wielding sadistic
clowns in the boiling heat of the Florida sun
wearing rubber masks sticking to their skin, barely
able to see
anything out of the eye holes.

They
stirred in me a sense of solitude,
each of them
enclosed in their masks of
self-imposed sensory
deprivation
tipping them over into the pornographic imagination
of terror: a tradition
that began with
Marquis de Sade in solitary confinement penning
The 120 Days of Sodom
with nothing but blood and sperm to make the quill
wet. In his footsteps,

the clowns, leaping with phallic velocity
over the edge into the golden cruelty of being anti-human;
their cold hands gripping the necks
and thighs and genitals, cutting into the limbs,
but they remained
muted in

their masks, not falling into De Sade's
endless philosophising
on the nature of a/morality
dragging the prose down. I,

into a
memory of
seeing a clown in Northampton, who
just stood alone on
the roadside holding a
handful of balloons. *The Guardian* speculated it was
Alan
Moore,
who
firmly denied it, pulling out
a series of train tickets from his bootleg jeans
to prove he was nowhere near,
but the clown had a copy of *The Satanic Bible*
popping out of his back pocket:
a book I read when I was 15.

It was
in shrink-wrap
in the Croydon branch of Waterstones. I

had to lie
and say I was 21 so the cardigan wearing Christian
would sell it to me
. As I left, I heard him on the phone. 'Yeah, I just sold it

to some wannabe serial killer; he had that look in his eyes. I bet
we'll see him on the front page of *The Sun*
after he commits matricide; a real-life Norman Bates
.' I

was about to interrupt and shout out,
that was the Butcher of Plainfield, but I didn't.
I just exited the shop
pulling the book out of the plastic finding
on
page 3 –

the drawing of Baphomet –

the goat's head/the huge breasts
/the caduceus erection/the yogic position – an androgynous
Satan – the figure

I saw in my dreams;
in the mirror I stared into attempting to learn how

to smile

but I felt nothing
except chaos – the chaos of body parts
throwing themselves into every kind of monstrosity – the kind
I dared to be, the monster
who was also sublime. I

waxed
my body, splattering body paints, wearing faux-
leather corsets,
see-through knickers, and
PVC cowboy boots. It was and wasn't fetishism; it was and wasn't
sexuality; it was and wasn't perversion; first was the vision,
the one in my head,
the one I saw across my body, my body morphing into
my androgynous Satanic self.

I was
my own mother; I had created myself,

out of love,

or the desire to be something other than
this pathetic human,
this pathetic male, that

I

saw in shop windows, me, standing there
in a t-shirt and jeans, hardly shaven, heavily
stoned, slightly
dead, that expression
of some teenager
who disappeared, whose face was
posted on every lamppost, falling
onto the rain drenched pavement.

I was never lost
but lost, never a rent boy, never had the sense
to charge, I fucked and was broke, like every
lost soul. I

was too
much in the images
of my own head to see any sense
of reality, but as we all know,

REALITY SUCKS,

spray-painting the words on a black canvas I burnt
in the back garden
as my neighbour took pictures with his Polaroid camera. I
was

alone
on my bed, seemingly
without any bones,
but somehow with a boner,
watching a Channel 4 documentary on
BD/SM showing a man
tied to a St Andrew's cross
having his left
nipple
pierced. I
could only dream

of being
a nun.

I, almost singing, 'Dennis Nilsen slept
with the dead, bathed the dead, dressed the dead, fucked the dead,
ate the dead,' as Dr Zoe Gemini glanced through
the Blast Press coffee table book,
Killing Confessions & Basement Crucifixions,

showing photos of
corpses side by side with the mugshots
of serial killers, making them seem
more human
than the victims.

As the kettle boiled, I placed three teabags into her oversized mug.
'Killing for them...'
I heard her voice without looking...
'is a process of consuming or assimilating...'
the mug slipped out of my hand...
'or imprisoning the souls of the victims inside their own heads...'
breaking on the floor.

She stopped and stared at me
as I stood perfectly still,
announcing the words I imagined scribbling
onto an A3 cardboard sheet,

'Do they really see (in the white of the eye)
the unveiling of the whole history of a life?'

She laughed,
'If you're unable empathise,
I guess your only chance is with a corpse.'

I felt tears as I bent down
to clear up the pieces with
a dustpan and brush.

     *

I went to see a spiritual healer
who pulled out a random card from his divination pack.
The card had a
photograph of him sitting in his own shit,
but he insisted
absolutely *it was* me,
even though *it was* so clearly him,
having his own name in capital letters under the image. 'I'm
not the one shitting here!' I screamed running

outside, almost suffocating. I slowed down, wandering into a
concrete
public space, sitting down on one of the uneven
benches, that were designed so the homeless
couldn't sleep on them.
I was wearing

nothing but cowboy boots,

as I was about to do a live art class at the Underworld,
where live art equalled nakedness
and a quick line of ketamine
to make the images
really real,

to embody

through my body –

their contours, their
unexpected,
alien presences. Marina looked
at me, at my image, at
the images
I scribbled and distilled
on A3 cardboard
sheets,
and she said, 'What else do you have?'

Whole body like gone.

– Samuel Beckett

Acknowledgements

Thank you to the editors of *The High Window*, *Nymphs & Thugs*, *South Bank Poetry* and *Zoo Zine*, where versions of a number of these poems first appeared, and to my friends, Nicki Heinen, Matthew Caley, Lydia Hounat and Peter Stickland for their feedback and support. Some poems were written as a part of the MA in Contemporary Performance Practices at the University of East London and were performed with Kesia Harriet Guillery and Marianna Turgunyan. I would also like to thank The Poetry School where I learnt to craft my work, and the open mic nights, Poetry Unplugged and Spoken Word London, where I first found my voice. And, of course, a huge thank you to the wonderful Amy Acre and Jake Wild Hall for accepting, editing and publishing *The Death of a Clown*.

Other titles by Bad Betty Press

Solomon's World
Jake Wild Hall

Unremember
Joel Auterson

In My Arms
Setareh Ebrahimi

The Story Is
Kate B Hall

The Dizziness Of Freedom
Edited by Amy Acre
and Jake Wild Hall

I'm Shocked
Iris Colomb

Ode to Laura Smith
Aischa Daughtery

The Pale Fox
Katie Metcalfe

TIGER
Rebecca Tamás

Forthcoming in 2019:

While I Yet Live
Gboyega Odubanjo

and more to be announced
on badbettypress.com